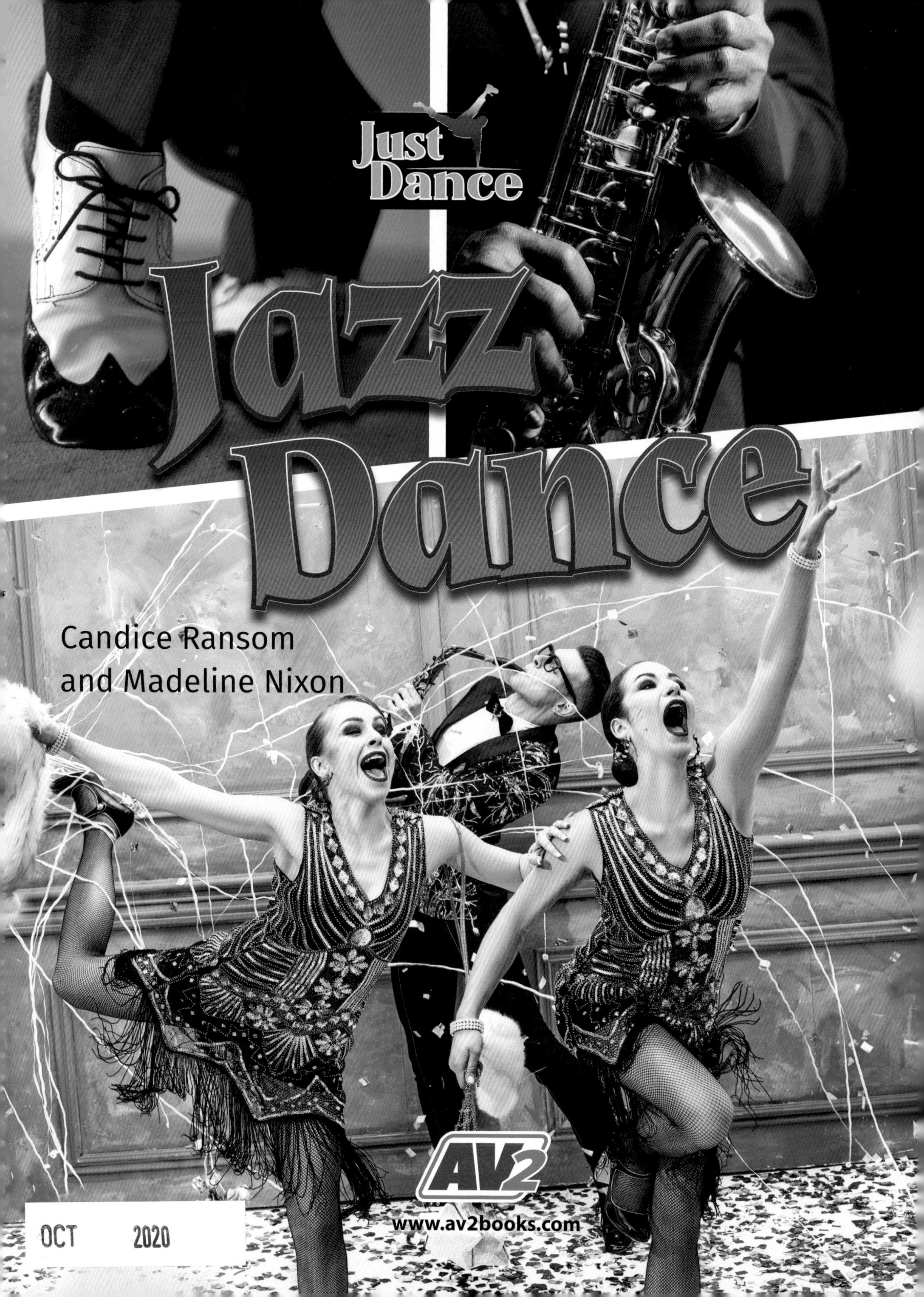
Just Dance
Jazz Dance
Candice Ransom
and Madeline Nixon
AV2
www.av2books.com

Step 1
Go to **www.av2books.com**

Step 2
Enter this unique code
JPIKE4UI1

Step 3
Explore your interactive eBook!

AV2 is optimized for use on any device

Your interactive eBook comes with...

Contents
Browse a live contents page to easily navigate through resources

Audio
Listen to sections of the book read aloud

Videos
Watch informative video clips

Weblinks
Gain additional information for research

Try This!
Complete activities and hands-on experiments

Key Words
Study vocabulary, and complete a matching word activity

Quizzes
Test your knowledge

Slideshows
View images and captions

... and much, much more!

Contents

Chapter 1

American Music, American Dance

The curtain rises. Five dancers are standing still. Then a lively song begins. The dancers step to the side, snapping their fingers. Suddenly they leap into the air. They land like cats. Their jazz dance is just getting started!

Jazz is influenced by many different styles of dance.

Jazz dance is based on jazz music. This music began around 1900 in New Orleans, Louisiana. Many people from Europe and West Africa lived there. Each group had its own culture in the United States. Europeans came with instruments such as pianos and trumpets. Africans added **upbeat** rhythms. When combined, a new kind of music was born.

But people did more than just listen to jazz. They also danced to it. They hopped, twisted, and twirled to the peppy music. This led to new dancing styles. These included tap and swing dancing.

Dance Tip

Make sure to warm up before a dance class. Jogging in place or jumping jacks are good warm-ups.

Jazz brought new rhythms. These rhythms promoted new forms of movement.

Jazz dancing is common in musicals.

At first, these dances were all called jazz dance. That changed in the 1950s. Jazz dance became a smoother style. It also became a performance dance. That is why jazz dance is most often seen in **Broadway** shows and movie musicals. Today's jazz dance uses movements from ballet, tap, and modern dance styles.

Chicago, a musical that features jazz dance, is the **SECOND LONGEST** running show on Broadway. It had more than **9,000** performances.

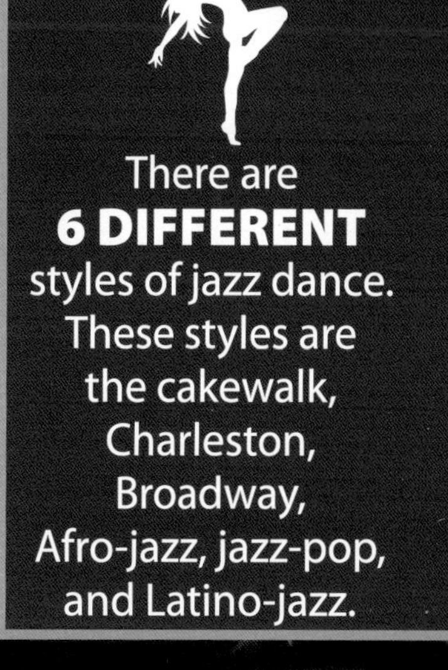

There are **6 DIFFERENT** styles of jazz dance. These styles are the cakewalk, Charleston, Broadway, Afro-jazz, jazz-pop, and Latino-jazz.

Jazz Timeline

Jazz dance is one of the most popular styles of dance in the United States. It began in the 1700s, but became more popular during the **Jazz Age** of the 1920s. What is known as jazz now is heavily influenced by this time period. Jazz appears in Broadway shows, dance movies, and even in musician's performances.

1700s

Africans were brought to the United States as slaves. They created their own unique culture that included dance.

1800s

The dances slaves created became more popular through **vaudeville** and other shows.

1923

The Charleston is introduced and becomes a key dance of the Jazz Age.

Jazz dance is a fun way to get moving.

1954

Bob Fosse creates groundbreaking jazz choreography for a Broadway play called *The Pajama Game*.

1980s

Musicians such as Madonna and Michael Jackson incorporate jazz dance into their acts.

Today

Jazz competitions and shows are very common. In 2005, *So You Think You Can Dance* debuted on American television. This dance competition features jazz as one of its styles.

Chapter 2

Clothes Make the Dance

Jazz dancers wear clothing that lets them move easily. Jazz pants are common. They are stretchy and loose at the ankle. Women often wear a **leotard** and tights. Men might wear a simple T-shirt.

Jazz dancers often wear matching costumes for performances.

The right shoes are important. Jazz shoes are made of soft leather. They let the dancer's foot flex. Stiff shoes do not work well. They make it hard to jump. Jazz shoes have a smooth, round patch on the bottom. It lets dancers turn quickly. Some jazz shoes are lace-up style. Others are slip-ons.

On stage, jazz dancers perform in **costumes**. The costumes are fun. Hats and gloves can be used. So can canes. Sparkles and glitter show off the dancers' moves.

Dance Tip

Some dancers prefer tights. Tights help keep your muscles warm.

Jazz dancers will occasionally go barefoot to better grip the floor.

Dancers can do isolations with their hands, heads, hips, ribs, or shoulders.

Chapter 3

Steppin' Out

Jazz dance is a high-energy style. Dancers move their whole bodies. But you can also do **isolations**. For example, hold your arms out. Then shift your hips from side to side. Do not move any other body part. This movement isolates your hips.

Isolations are combined with steps. You can step forward with your right foot in a jazz walk. At the same time, your left shoulder moves up. The shoulder isolation adds flair to the movement.

Certain moves set jazz dance apart from other types of dance. The fingers of a jazz dancer are often spread wide. That is called jazz hands. Fast, little kicks forward are called flick kicks.

Dance Tip

Practice doing isolations in front of a mirror. Keep other parts of your body still.

Jazz hands can easily be added to any jazz choreography.

Jazz dancing is great exercise.

A grapevine is a popular step. First, you step to your right. Then your left leg crosses behind your right foot and taps down. **Chassé** is a move borrowed from ballet. You step out to the right. Then you slide your left foot to meet your right foot. This step is performed moving quickly across the floor.

Turning, jumping, and leaping are harder moves. They make jazz dance exciting to watch.

Dance Tip

Take time after class to stretch your muscles. Stretching helps prevent injury.

Try It Out

Jazz Square

This four-step move follows the shape of a square. Start with your feet together.

1. Bring your right foot across your left foot. Your legs will be crossed.
2. Next, step back with your left foot. Your weight will be on your left foot.
3. Step your right leg out to the right side.
4. Finally, swing your left foot in front of your right foot. Now you're ready to do another jazz square!

Becoming a star takes a lot of practice.

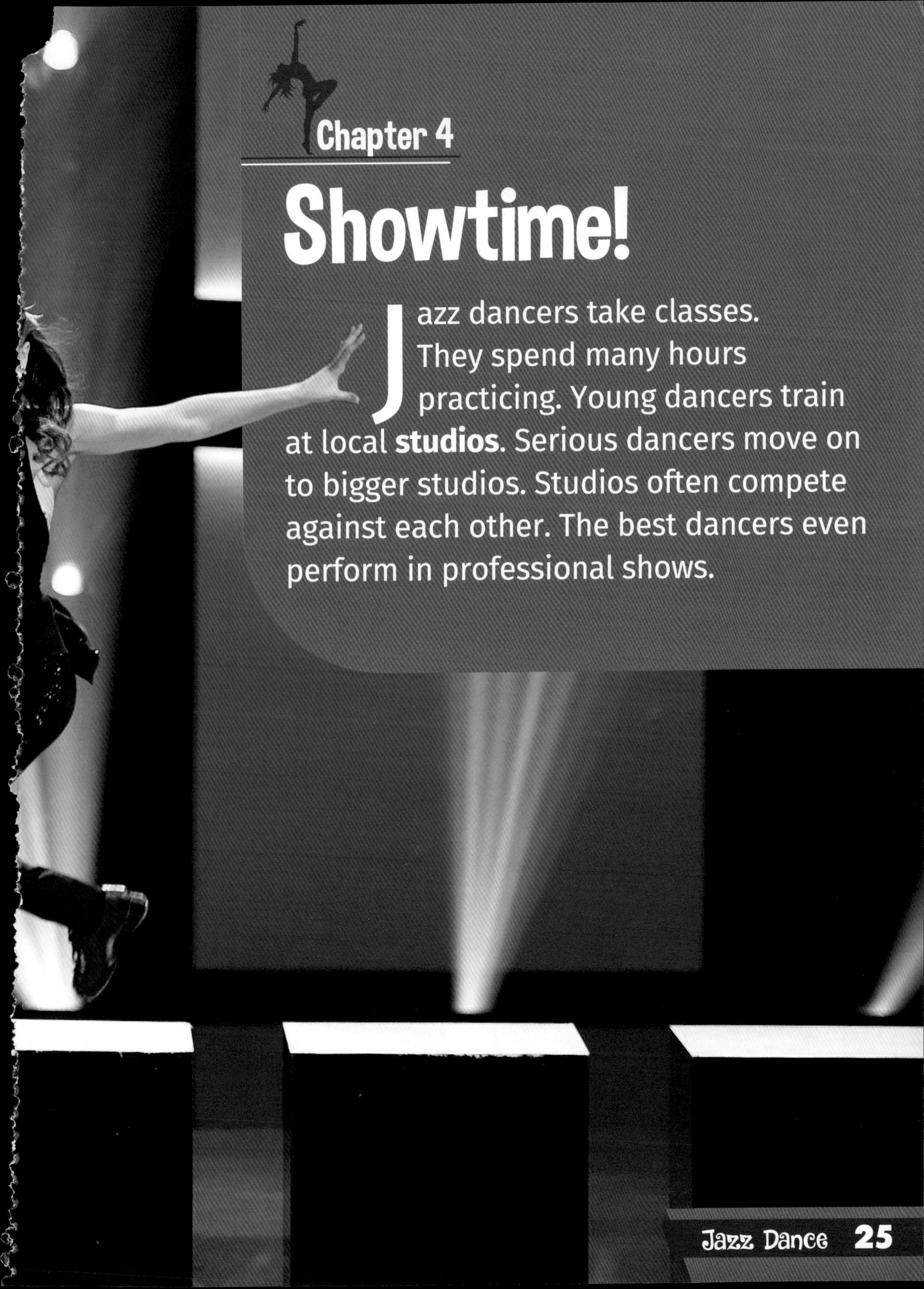

Chapter 4

Showtime!

Jazz dancers take classes. They spend many hours practicing. Young dancers train at local **studios**. Serious dancers move on to bigger studios. Studios often compete against each other. The best dancers even perform in professional shows.

To get a job in a show, dancers **audition**. Many dancers might try out for the same job. They give a short performance for the people running the show. If a dancer passes the audition, he or she is hired.

Many dancers want to be in a Broadway show. But there are other jobs for dancers.

Dancers can work on a cruise ship. Cruise ships are large boats. People take trips on them for vacation. The ships often provide entertainment for the passengers. Dancers **rehearse** most days and perform in live shows. They also get to visit new places.

Dance Tip

If you can, take a dance class in a different style, along with jazz dance lessons. Successful jazz dancers take classes in ballet, modern dance, and hip-hop.

Many jazz dancers yearn to perform in shows.

Theme parks also need dancers. A cast of dancers will put on shows every day. Other jobs include dancing in movies, TV commercials, and music videos. Many dancers tour with singers or bands. Jazz dancers also compete on TV talent shows.

There are **ONLY 28 DANCE COMPANIES** worldwide that **SOLELY FOCUS** on **JAZZ DANCE**.

The record for the world's largest contemporary jazz dance lesson was set on **NOVEMBER 19, 2017**. There were **589 PEOPLE** who joined.

Professional jazz dancers may find themselves dancing in Broadway shows that feature jazz dance, such as *Chicago*.

Quiz

1 Which jazz move is borrowed from ballet?

2 How did people from West Africa help create jazz music?

3 What are jazz hands?

4 Where can jazz dancers work that allows them to travel to new places?

5 What fun additions can be a part of jazz dancers costumes?

6 How many people were a part of the world record jazz dance class?

7 What is it called when a dancer only moves one part of his or her body?

8 What was the Broadway show Bob Fosse created groundbreaking choreography for in 1964?

9 Why do stiff shoes not work well in jazz dance?

10 Which dance styles have influenced current jazz dance?

ANSWERS

1. Chassé **2.** New rhythms promoted new forms of movement. **3.** Spread fingers during a jazz step **4.** Cruise ship **5.** Hats, gloves, and canes **6.** 589 **7.** Isolations **8.** *The Pajama Game* **9.** They make it hard to jump. **10.** Ballet, tap, and modern dance